SPORTS PAGE

0 43422 69522 5

The Sports Page

Compiled by Dale Tobias

Copyright 1997, Great Quotations

ISBN# 1-56245-039-5

Great Quotations Publishing Inc.
1967 Quincy Court
Glendale Heights, IL 60139
Printed in Hong Kong

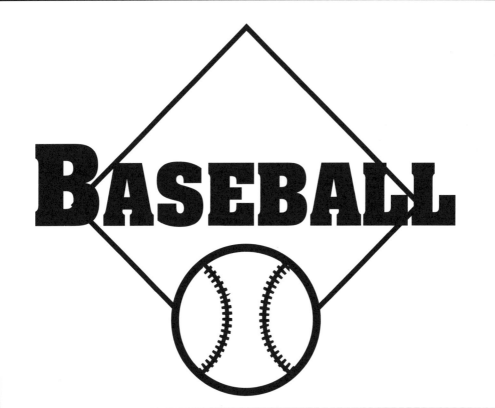

"**B**aseball is the belly button of society. Straighten out baseball and you'll straighten out the rest of the world."

Former big league pitcher Bill (Spaceman) Lee,
on life as he sees it.

"**W**hen he gets down in a crouch, it sounds like a bowl of Rice Krispies."

White Sox pitcher Greg Hibbard, on catcher Carlton Fisk, who had surgery on both knees.

"**The** first time I came into a game there, I got into the bullpen car and they told me to lock the doors."

Orioles pitcher Mike Flanagan, a veteran of 16 major league seasons, on playing in New York.

6

"**W**riters like to say they've seen a lot of players come and go. I've seen a lot of writers come and go."

Rangers pitcher Nolan Ryan, in his 25th major league season.

"**G**et an intentional walk."

Nolan Ryan, on what he hasn't done in baseball.

8

"**I saw him throw two no-hitters when I was a kid. Nearly 20 years later, he's getting me out.**"

Detroit Tigers outfielder Rob Deer, who was 0 for 14 lifetime against Nolan Ryan, on the longevity of the 45-year-old Texas pitcher.

"**If he had made me a consultant five minutes ago, my first recommendation would have been not to fire the manager.**"

Former Royals manager John Wathan, on being offered a job as a consultant immediately after he was fired by General Manager Herk Robinson.

10

"**I feel like a guy in an open casket at his own funeral. Everyone walks by and says what a good guy you were. But it doesn't do you any good. You're still dead.**"

Tom Trebelhorn, fired recently as Milwaukee Brewers manager, on what it feels like.

11

"**B**ack then, if you had a sore arm, the only people concerned were you and your wife. Now it's you, your wife, your agent, your investment counselor, your stockbroker and your publisher."

Former big league pitcher Jim Bouton, on how the game has changed since he played.

12

"**I** found out that it's not good to talk about my troubles. Eighty percent of the people who hear them don't care and the other twenty percent are glad you're having trouble."

Tom Lasorda, Los Angeles Dodgers manager, on burdening others.

"**I**f you don't believe in yourself, everyone knows it. How can you lead the cavalry if you think you look funny sitting on a horse?"

Hal McRae, manager of the Kansas City Royals, on leadership.

"**B**eing an umpire is like being a king. It prepares you for nothing."

Ron Luciano, retired American League umpire, on his former profession.

15

"**I thought I had it. I was twisting like this. It grazed my glove, hit me in the head and bounced over. I'll be on ESPN for about a month. Anybody got a Band-Aid?"**

Jose Canseco, after Carlos Martinez's fly ball bounced off his head over the fence for a home run.

"I'm a baseball player."

Ryan Thompson, of the New York Mets, when asked what kind of player he was?

17

"**The** motto of the team I played with was 'win or else.' I don't know what the 'else' meant, and I never wanted to learn."

Pitcher Chuck Cary, in camp with the White Sox, on playing in Japan.

18

"**E**rrors are a part of baseball, but Abner Doubleday was a jerk for inventing them."

Texas Ranger second baseman Bill Ripken.

"**B**ecause of the proximity of the San Andreas fault, when the quake hits, maybe Candlestick will absorb it all and the rest of the area will be safe."

Pirates outfielder Andy Van Slyke, who dislikes playing at Candlestick Park.

20

"**W**hen I threw, I only heard my elbow go 'snap' and 'crackle.' I didn't hear it go 'pop'—and that's good."

Cleveland Indian pitcher Mike Bielecki, after testing his sore right elbow.

"**H**ey, you are only young once.

But you can be immature forever."

Veteran relief pitcher Larry Andersen.

"**H**e always said that if you feel like you're going to hit into a double play, strike out."

Colorado Rockies manager Don Baylor recalling some wisdom from Earl Weaver.

"In the '70s I threw in the 90s; in the '90s I throw in the 70s."

Thirty-nine-year-old Frank Tanana, of the Mets, on his evolution as a pitcher.

24

"It actually giggles at you as it goes by."

Ex-Cub Rick Monday, recalling Phil Niekro's knuckleball.

"**In the seventh inning, (the fans) all get up and sing, 'Take Me Out to the Ballgame', and they're already there. It's really a stupid thing to say.**"

Phillies reliever Larry Anderson on playing the Chicago Cubs in Wrigley Field.

"After he hit me, I told him, 'Hey, dude, you're on the wrong field for this kind of contact. We need some yard markers.'"

Los Angeles Dodgers first baseman Kal Daniels, after a collision in the base paths with Deion Sanders of the Atlanta Braves and Falcons.

"**R**un it out, you piece of crud."

Carlton Fisk to Deion Sanders.

"**I**'d never been that scared before in my life. Baseball, salaries ... nothing else mattered. I wanted to tell my wife that I loved her. I wanted to tell my kids that I loved them. I once told my wife that if anything happened to me, find a man who would treat my kids like I would treat them. That night, I got selfish. I didn't want anyone else raising my three sons."

Bo Jackson, designated hitter for the White Sox, after the team's charter plane blew an engine and had to make an emergency landing in Des Moines, Iowa.

"**I** believe **ESPN** has widely used baseball to dominate cable programming throughout the summer. There are only so many tractor pulls and billiard matches you can televise."

Fay Vincent, ex-baseball commissioner on being sympathetic to the TV networks' reports of large losses but not thinking that CBS and ESPN were total losers.

30

"**O**ver the shoulder punches carry a heavy fine in the **NBA**. So I'll swing at the stomach, the guy will fall and I won't get fined."

Miami Heat center Rony Seikaly, on his working with boxing trainer Angelo Dundee to improve his footwork, agility and balance on the basketball court.

"**What security? Security is how many years you have on your contract when you're fired.**"

Frank Hamblen, ex-coach of the NBA's Milwaukee Bucks, on job security.

"We're going to be exciting—of course, it was exciting when the Titanic went down."

Bob Weiss, ex-coach of the NBA's Atlanta Hawks, on his team.

"**T**here's always been the sense of: 'There's something about this guy, I don't like him, I don't trust him.' There's always been the sense that I'm up to something, but if I was up to something, wouldn't I be through with it by now?"

Isiah Thomas, star guard for the NBA's Detroit Pistons, on his image.

"I told them I didn't think we would have won that game without the plane."

Dick Motta, coach of the NBA's Sacramento Kings who were 1-40 on the road one season, on being asked by club owners to justify the use of a charter plane.

"We put it all together.

Unfortunately, everything was bad."

Jimmy Rogers, former coach of the NBA's Minnesota Timberwolves who had the league's worst record, after a loss.

37

"**W**e can't win at home and we can't win on the road. My problem as general manager is I can't think of another place to play."

Pat Williams, general manager of the NBA's Orlando Magic, during his team's 17 game losing streak.

"I don't care how good you are.
I'm still the No. 1 draft pick."

Shaquille O'Neal, former collegiate star center for LSU's basketball team, to Arizona center Sean Rooks after Rooks outplayed O'Neal badly in the Wildcats' win over the Tigers.

"I don't read the stories about myself. I just look at the pictures."

Shaquille O'Neal of the Orlando Magic, on how he handles the acclaim.

" **I**'ve always said, if you don't play for the Celtics, you're not playing pro basketball."

Larry Bird, after Boston's first-round pick, Jon Barry, was traded to the Milwaukee Bucks.

"**W**ouldn't Alaa Abdelnaby be a great clue for Wheel of Fortune, especially if you weren't allowed to buy a vowel?"

Unknown

"Basketball is like church.

Many attend but few understand."

Scott Skiles, Orlando Magic, guard, dismissing the fans' booing of him.

43

"**W**hen he sits down, his ears pop."

Don Nelson, Golden State Warrior general manager and coach, on Shawn Bradley, the 7 ft. 6 in. former BYU center.

44

"**We** played basketball Monday through Saturday. If you went Monday through Friday and had avoided getting into a fight, you didn't go on Saturday because it was going to be your time. That's the way you should learn to play basketball ... the tough way first. You can get the fundamentals later."

Larry Johnson, star player for the NBA's Charlotte Hornets, on how he learned to play basketball while growing up in a tough section of Dallas.

"**T**here is a 'D' in Woolridge, but it's silent."

John Salley when asked how ex-teammate
Orlando Woolridge plays defense.

"**A**bility may get you to the top, but it takes character to keep you there."

John Wooden, former UCLA basketball coach.

"**T**he more Final Fours you go to, the more cousins you find out you have who need tickets."

Mike Krzyzewski, Duke basketball coach, on his team playing in its fifth consecutive Final Four and the problems that creates.

"**I remember people digging up grass from my front yard, putting it in a bag and leaving.**"

Chris Webber, former basketball player at the University of Michigan, on being idolized as a prepster.

"This is a great school. Look at all the alumni who are in the NBA."

Brian Reese, basketball player at North Carolina, assessing the university.

"We will use a Clarence Thomas defense—we deny everything."

Tom Asbury, Pepperdine basketball coach, on what kind of defense his team will employ.

"**T**hings got so bad that I had to play my student manager for a while. They got really bad when she started to complain to the press that she wasn't getting enough playing time."

Linda Hill-McDonald, basketball coach for the University of Minnesota women's team, on squad's 6-22 season.

"**We have black players, we have white players, a Mormon point guard and four Yugoslavs. Our toughest decision isn't what offense or defense to run, but what type of warmup music to play.**"

Wagner coach Tim Capstraw on the problems with going well beyond the New York city limits to recruit players at the Staten Island school.

RULES JORDAN

"**I** knew I would be going places and I just wanted to know where I was when I got there."

Michael Jordan, on why he was a geography major at North Carolina.

54

"**P**re-season is just a way to screw fans out of money."

Charles Barkley, when asked to compare pre-season play to regular-season games.

BARKLEY

BARKINGS

RULES

JORDAN

"**I** have a right to associate with whomever I choose to. This [gambling report] is not a Pete Rose matter."

Michael Jordan, Chicago Bulls guard on reports he lost money while playing golf.

56

"Mark Jackson says that he loves his fiancee so much he would give up basketball for her. Not me. I love my wife (Maureen), but she doesn't pay the bills like **NBA** money can."

Charles Barkley claiming that New York Knick guard Mark Jackson has his priorities out of order.

BARKLEY

BARKINGS

"**I know my place. Let's put it this way: If I've got an open 8-footer and [Jordan's] got an open 10-footer, I'll pass it to Mike.**"

Larry Johnson, on protocol in 1993 NBA All-Star Game.

"**I consider it a great opportunity on my part to work with a distinguished actor. He is great at acting.**"

Barkley responding to a question regarding his promotional spot for a new movie, "Hot Shots," which he did with Detroit's Bill Laimbeer.

"**For $58,000, I'd have liked to hit him more than once.**"

Michael Jordan, who was fined $10,000 and suspended for one game, at a cost of $48,000, after fighting with Reggie Miller.

"**U**s Nike guys are loyal to Nike because they pay us a lot of money ... I have two million reasons not to wear Reebok."

Barkley on why he wears Nike shoes.

61

BARKINGS

"**I**t's nice to play against him.

Sometimes you get your picture in the

paper."

Seattle forward Eddie Johnson, on playing against Michael Jordan.

" **A**n education is a wonderful thing, unless you can run and jump over buildings."

Barkley was asked if it didn't seem a bit odd that seven of the nine NBA players involved in the Stay in School public-service campaign left college early for the NBA, including himself.

BARKLEY

BARKINGS

RULES JORDAN

"**I** was looking at that **McDonald's** commercial, and he probably really can make that shot off the **Sears Tower** ... nothing but net."

New York Knicks guard Doc Rivers, on the Chicago Bulls' Michael Jordan.

"**J**apan makes the best car; Italians make the best clothes. Why can't we be the best at something, too?"

Barkley responding to complaints about the Dream team's domination of the competition.

RULES

JORDAN

"**T**o those who wonder whether I can coach or not, I taught Michael Jordan how to jump."

Eddie Fogler, who recently left Vanderbilt to coach South Carolina.

"**The more attention he gets, the less I have to deal with the nitwits in the media.**"

Charles Barkley on why he isn't jealous of rookie Shaquille O'Neal.

BARKLEY

BARKINGS

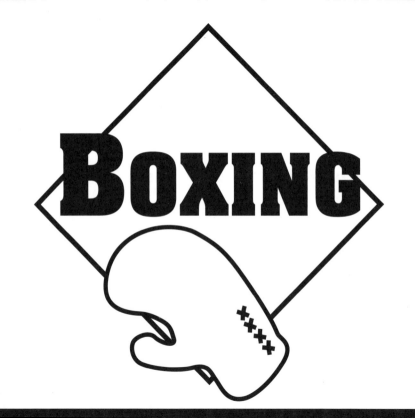

"**I don't try to intimidate anybody before a fight. That's nonsense. I intimidate people by hitting them.**"

Former heavyweight champion Mike Tyson, on his approach to a bout.

"**For years I've been telling people I was pretty good. But I've never been one to brag.**"

Former heavyweight champion Muhammad Ali.

"That will be a battle of the Ben-Gay."

Boxer George Foreman, 44, on the possibility of a fight with ex-champion Larry Holmes, 42.

"**I've been doing this for 25 years. It's kind of hard after you finish. What does a writer do after he's finished? He goes to a bar and starts thinking about something to write.**"

Former heavyweight champion Larry Holmes, on coming out of retirement at 41 to resume boxing.

72

"**H**e (Chavez) speaks English, Spanish and he's bilingual, too."

Promoter Don King, talking about Julio Ceasar Chavez's pay-per-view fight against Greg Haugen in Mexico City.

"**N**obody is talked about more than me. I am the best promoter in the world. And I say that humbly."

Boxing promoter Don King.

"**I**f you walk down the street and get into a fight, you don't have time to look at a tape."

James "Buddy" McGirt, on why he doesn't find viewing tapes helpful before a fight.

"**H**e's made a career of beating senior citizens and Jenny Craig dropouts."

Mike Lupica, speaking on ESPN's "The Sports Reporters" about former heavyweight champion Evander Holyfield.

BROADCAST BLIPS

RADIO

" **The only mystery in life is why kamikaze pilots wore helmets.**"

CBS-TV commentator Al McGuire.

"**T**he intelligence of any manager is magnified in proportion to the failure of the other team's bullpen."

Bernie Lincicome of the Chicago Tribune, *writing about baseball.*

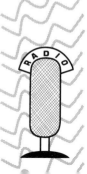

"**A** baseball player saying, 'You know, I oughta be curing cancer for the money they're paying me to hit .245.'"

John Eisenberg, sports columnist for the Baltimore Sun, *on one thing he would like to hear.*

80

"**I**t's kind of scary that they give the Marines guns if they don't know which end of a maple leaf is up."

Carol Cole of the Toronto Star, *after a U.S. Marine color guard displayed the Canadian flag upside down before Game 2 of the World Series.*

81

"Until recently, I thought the luge was something that happened to your car after **15,000 miles."**

CBS sportscaster James Brown on the Winter Olympics.

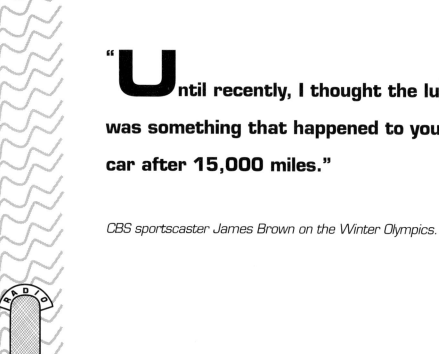

"**My uncle always describes an unforced error as his first marriage.**"

From television tennis commentator Bud Collins.

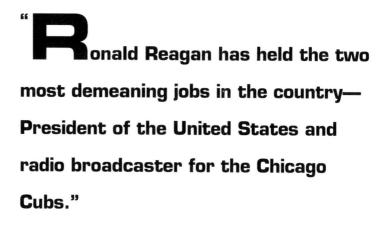

"**Ronald Reagan has held the two most demeaning jobs in the country— President of the United States and radio broadcaster for the Chicago Cubs.**"

George Will, columnist, author and long-suffering Chicago Cubs baseball fan.

"**The best thing about the College World Series is Dick Vitale is not here.**"

ESPN announcer Mike Patrick, on being assigned to the College World Series.

"**M**oney is the driving force in college sports. If **NBC** tells Notre Dame to kick off at 3, all they ask is, 'A.M. or P.M.?'"

*ESPN commentator Beano Cook, on Notre Dame's
$37 million contract with NBC to televise all Irish football
games for the next five seasons.*

86

"If I was playing today, I'd be a million-dollar player. Is that scary, or what?"

Baseball announcer Bob Uecker, ex-catcher with a 200 career batting average.

"**Twelve for 23 ... it doesn't take a genius to see that's under 50 percent.**"

ABC-TV commentator Dick Vitale, while at a Duke-UCLA game.

"**I**'m not into hyping guys, but Duke's Grant Hill could succeed Michael Jordan as the next true superstar in the NBA."

CBS-TV announcer Jim Nantz

" **They won't need to order any gold medals. Just melt down Deion Sander's jewelry.**"

Radio personality Dave Coombs of Albany, N.Y., linking flashy Atlanta Falcons cornerback and the 1996 summer Olympics Games in Atlanta.

"**Football is to baseball as blackjack is to bridge. One is the quick jolt; the other the deliberate, slow paced game of skill.**"

Announcer Vin Scully.

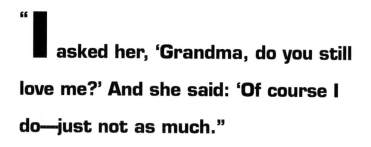

"**I asked her, 'Grandma, do you still love me?' And she said: 'Of course I do—just not as much.**"

Tom Witosky, sports reporter for the Des Moines Register, *whose story was critical of the University of Iowa, that upset his grandmother.*

"**A**t the beginning, he was very much against it, but by the time I was 16 I was making more money than he was."

Oddsmaker Jimmy "The Greek" Snyder, when asked if his father had ever warned him against the evils of gambling.

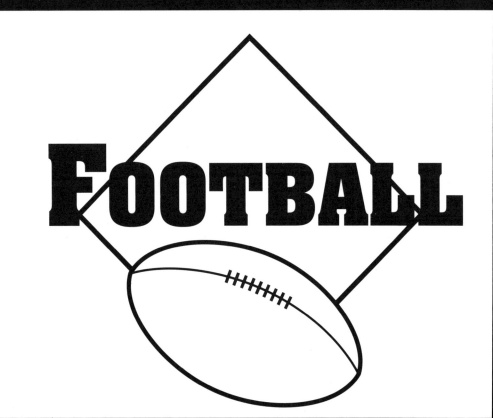

"**F**ootball is blood, tears, sweat, pain. If you want something else, go to a chess match."

Chicago Bears coach Mike Ditka.

"It's really chaotic. Everyone grabs at each other and then they all fall down."

Novice fan Ding Jinghus, after watching Pacific Lutheran University of Tacoma, Wash., defeat Evangel College of Springfield Mo., 20-7, in the first football game in China.

"**E**very night, I tell myself, I'm gonna dream about my girl. I'm gonna dream about my girl. But it's always hamhocks."

Dallas Cowboys guard Nate Newton, on the difficulty of losing weight.

97

"**That's the way kids are today. They talk more. Maybe it has something to do with all that rapping.**"

Chicago veteran linebacker Mike Singletary, commenting on the verbal jousting that occurred before the Bears met Atlanta.

"I heard things about my mother I never heard before."

Deion Sanders, defensive back for the NFL's Atlanta Falcons, on the Los Angeles Raiders' talkative wideouts.

"He probably would have said, 'What the hell's a woman doing on the field?'"

Marie Lombardi, widow of Vince Lombardi, when asked what her husband's reaction would have been to her role as the honoree designated to toss the coin before Super Bowl XV.

"**When you don't fit into the computer on things like size, speed and vertical jump, you are basically a reject. You are a possession receiver. A possession receiver is a polite term for SLOW.**"

Bears wide receiver Tom Waddle, who has caught on in the NFL after being cut three times.

101

"**I guess since no one wants me, I'll go home and watch 'The Young and Restless' on television.**"

Running back Mike Rozier, after being waived by the Houston Oilers.

102

"You have to understand that what you read in the newspapers is not always gospel. Certainly, Matthew, Mark, Luke and John do not work for the papers in the San Diego area."

Dan Henning, coach of the NFL's San Diego Chargers, on being under siege by the city's media for the team's 1-8 record.

"**He's in terrible shape. He threw up four or five times. I should've known better than to take anybody out of Detroit. You know damn well they ain't going to be in good enough shape to play. That's the reason they're 8-8 all the time.**"

Ex-Eagles coach Buddy Ryan on linebacker Paul Butcher, formerly of the Lions, after Butcher left practice one day because of the heat.

"**W**e've always said in the locker room that the reporters don't know anything. And he's just a reporter now."

*Lawrence Taylor, star linebacker for the NFL's
New York Giants, on the prediction by former coach
Bill Parcels, now an NBC-TV commentator, that the
Redskins would win the NFC East.*

"**It will go down as one of the worst trades in the past, present and future history of the NFL.**"

Irwin Jacobs, a part owner of the Minnesota Vikings, on the acquisition by former general manager Mike Lynn of Herschel Walker for five players and several draft choices.

"**Y**ou draw **X**'s and **O**'s on a blackboard and that's not so difficult. I can even do it with my left hand."

John McKay, former Southern Cal and Tampa Bay Buccaneer football coach, on his profession.

107

"**There** was a lot of emotion at the Alamo, and there were also a lot of dead people."

George Seifert, coach of the NFL's San Francisco 49ers,
on the difference between emotion and productivity.

"I never set out to hurt anyone deliberately ... unless, it was, you know, important—like a league game or something."

Dick Butkus, NFL Hall of Famer and former star linebacker for the Chicago Bears, on his pro career.

"**H**e was so good, everybody thought. Bill Walsh could coach. Of course, I knew better."

Jerry Glanville, coach of the NFL's Atlanta Falcons, on injured quarterback Joe Montana's value to the 49ers.

110

"**He's one man who didn't let success go to his clothes.**"

Mike Ditka, on former NFL coach now TV commentator John Madden.

111

"**H**e told me I cost him the $150 he was going to use to take his family on vacation. I'm thinking: 'Where are you going to take them, the movies?'"

Dallas's Leon Leti, on a fan's reaction to his Super Bowl fumble out of the end zone.

"Football is a cold, cold business, and it's even colder in New England."

Patriots linebacker Eugene Lockhart, on being traded from the Cowboys during the off-season.

"When they drive by, they wave and all their fingers show."

Detroit Lions coach Wayne Fontes, on his popularity with fans despite talk that his job might be in jeopardy.

"**H**is big concern when he retired was that he didn't have any hobbies. He didn't play golf. He didn't drive a sports car. He smoked cigarettes and ate donuts. Those were his hobbies. He had to decide if he'd have six cream-filled or seven cream-filled."

Joe Bugel. coach of the NFL's Phoenix Cardinals, on whether Bill Parcels will return to coaching.

"**L**ast year was a bummer being home early. My wife started making out a list of chores at midseason."

Simon Fletcher, defensive end for the NFL's Denver Bronco's, on looking forward to the playoffs after finishing with a 5-11 record the previous year.

"It sounds better than 'jerk.'"

George Seifert, after a reporter noted that he's been called 'evasive'.

"**I** was ooohing and aaahing about the brilliant (fall) colors the other day. My wife said, 'But, Ron, this happens every fall.'"

Ron Meyer, who was fired as coach of the NFL's winless Indianapolis Colts, on finding a whole new world.

118

"**If they had tightened up the immigration laws, I'd still be kicking.**"

Lou Groza, NFL Hall of Famer, on today's soccer-style kickers.

"**H**e's Edward Scissorhands.

He couldn't catch a cold in Alaska

buck-naked."

*Emmit Smith, Dallas running back, on teammate
Larry Brown, a defensive back.*

120

"**In my next life, I want to come back as a kicker, or some fat lady's poodle. It's basically the life.**"

Los Angeles Raiders defensive end Howie Long on kickers.

121

"**I told them if our offense can produce as well as they can, we'll be a good football team.**"

Wisconsin football Coach Barry Alvarez, whose staff of assistant coaches welcomed six babies into the world during the off-season.

"I needed one like this to help my stomach."

Auburn coach Pat Dye, who was hospitalized two weeks before with abdominal pains, after the Tigers' 56-6 victory over Vanderbilt.

"**It's going to be a football team that plays hard. I'm not going to promise a number of wins. If I could do that, I'd be Curley the Greek.**"

New Louisiana State football coach Curley Hallman, on what type of team he plans to field.

125

"**The** snap was good, the hold was good. I don't know what happened. But I heard the second thump awfully quick after I hit it. You hate to hear that sound."

Tennessee kicker Greg Burke after Alabama blocked a 50-yard field goal attempt.

"**A** NCAA rule says we have to have one day off each week. I just didn't think they'd take game day off."

John Gutekunst, Minnesota football coach, on his team's 58-0 loss to Colorado.

"**I set a lot of records at Notre Dame. Unfortunately, they were all the wrong kind.**"

Gerry Faust, University of Akron coach on his years as coach at Notre Dame.

"I can see now why Joe Paterno was the Sports Illustrated Sportsman of the Year."

New England Patriots coach Dick MacPherson, who continues to feud with the Penn State coach even after leaving Syracuse University. MacPherson was making reference to the Nittany Lions' 81-0 victory against Cincinnati during the Fall of 1991.

"**It's better to go 7-3 than 9-1. When you are 7-3, everybody talks about the games you won. When you are 9-1, all anyone talks about is the game you lost.**"

Some philosophy from Doug Dickey, former Florida football coach.

"8-0-3 ain't a record. It's an area code."

Jim Muldoon, the Pacific 10 Conference's public relations director, on Michigan having no defeats and three ties during the 1992 season.

"**I have a lifetime contract. The biggest games I ever coached were when I had a one year contract.**"

Bobby Bowden, coach of top-ranked Florida State football team, on how a game with No. 2 Miami will not be the biggest game he's coached.

"**If it was, Army and Navy would be playing for the national championship every year.**"

Bobby Bowden, Florida State football coach, when asked if discipline was the key to winning.

133

"**I** got me one of them rings. It reads, 'National champions 1991, '92, '93, '94, Love mother.'"

Bobby Bowden, who has not won a national championship despite 216 career wins, during a breakfast speech in Miami.

134

"I'm looking forward to the challenge of playing in the Big Eight."

Fullback Nicky Sualua of Santa Ana (Calif.) Mater Dei High, after commiting to Ohio State.

"I don't care what anyone says, Navy will be the surprise team in the country."

Notre Dame coach Lou Holtz, hyping an opponent that had a 1-10 record the previous year.

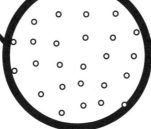

"**L**ife is like golf. If you keep in the fairway, you never have to ask for a ruling."

Professional golfer Chi Chi Rodriguez, on coping.

"**I** used to play with a guy who cheated so much that he once shot a hole in one and wrote zero on his scorecard."

Senior Tour golfer Bob Brue, on creative scorekeeping.

"**M**ORE."

Golfer Craig Stadler, asked how he's putting this year compared to 1982, when he won the Masters.

140

"**I told [a Masters official] I was getting too old to play, but he kept saying, 'Gene, they don't want to see you play, they just want to see if you're still alive.'"**

Gene Sarazen, 90, on being tired of his role as one of the Masters; honorary starters.

"**I** asked my caddie for a sand wedge and **10** minutes later he came back with a ham on rye."

Chi Chi Rodriguez on his Puerto Rican accent.

"**S**till your shot."

Dave Marr, TV commentator and former PGA player,
on the three ugliest words in golf.

143

"**S**o she pulled out a $5 bill and handed it over. I wrote a nice, personal, little note in the margin and signed it. She thanked me profusely. 'I'll treasure this the rest of my life.' A half-hour later, paying my tab with a $20 bill, I got that $5 bill back in change."

Pro golfer Lee Trevino—noting how some athletes are refusing to give autographs unless they think the recipient wants to keep them—remembers when he refused to sign a napkin for a woman in a coffee shop.

"**They call it golf because all the other four-letter words were taken.**"

Raymond Floyd, after falling out of contention at the British Open.

"**I**t is a game whose aim is to hit a very small ball into an even smaller hole, with weapons singularly ill-designed for that purpose."

Winston Churchill, on golf.

"**I'll take a two-stroke penalty, but I'll be damned if I'm going to play the ball where it lies.**"

Pro golfer Elaine Johnson's reaction after her tee shot hit a tree and caromed into her bra.

"**Y**ou know you're on the senior tour when your back goes out more than you do."

Senior PGA Tour player Bob Brue.

"**T**he alligator sleeps all day. He lives to be 150. I sleep at least 10 hours a day. The turtle moves at a slow pace and lives to be a 200. I walk—and not too fast."

Chi Chi Rodriguez, 57, credits his longevity in golf to learning lessons from nature.

"**I** had a lot more hair then—and it was a different color."

Raymond Floyd, on what has changed since he won his first golf tournament in 1963.

"**I** think hitting a golf ball is insane because you have to go chase it. But when you lift a weight and put it down, it's still there at your feet."

U.S. Olympic weightlifter Rich Schutz on golf.

"**G**ive me golf clubs, fresh air and a beautiful partner—and you can keep my golf clubs and the fresh air."

Jack Benny on golf.

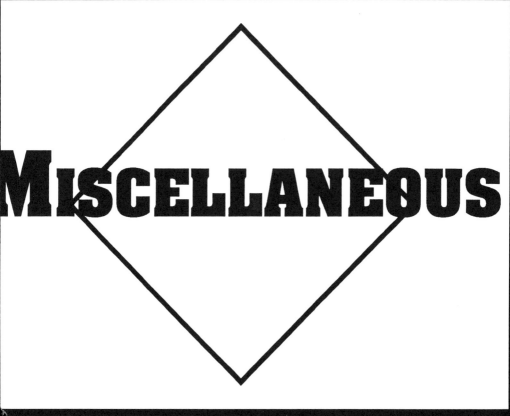

MISCELLANEOUS

"**I** just got back from court where I had my name officially changed to Willy T. McRibbs."

Willy T. Ribbs, the first black driver to qualify for the Indianapolis 500, on McDonald's 11th-hour decision to sponsor his car.

"**I'm a typical Hoosier. I grew up dribbling a basketball around a 2 1/2-mile race track.**"

Indianapolis native Bill Pappas, who is 6'7" and an engineer on Jim Hall's Indy team.

"**J**ust when it looked like our boys would break into the top 84 at the next Winter Games."

Scott Ostler of the San Francisco Chronicle, *reacting to the news that the U.S. Bobsled Team was in financial trouble.*

"**Umpiring is best described as the profession of standing between two 7-year-olds with one ice cream cone.**"

Former umpire Ron Luciano.

"**O**nce I start to run, I forget what I have on my feet, anyway. Whoops, there goes the endorsement."

Holli Hyche, Indiana State sprinter, after winning the women's 100 and 200 in the NCAA championships in borrowed shoes.

"**I**'ve told Nathalie she can't have the baby on a game night. I'm not going to miss a playoff game."

Mario Lemieux, whose fiancee, Nathalie Asselin, was due to give birth the next week.

"I stopped more than I let go past. I feel good about that."

Janet Chakunda, goalie for the Zimbabwe women's field hockey team, which lost all seven of its games in the recent World University Games by an aggregate score of 107-0.

"**The horse weighs 1,000 pounds and I weigh 95. I guess I better get him to cooperate.**"

Jockey, Steve Cauthen.

"Anonymity is having your name printed 8,000 times a week and people still don't know who you are."

Anonymous

" **I** spent 12 years training for a career that was over in a week. Joe spent one week training for a career that lasted 12 years."

Bruce Jenner, former Olympic decathlon champion, when asked to compare himself to former NFL quarterback Joe Namath.

"Do you have any problems, other than that you're unemployed and a moron and a dork."

John McEnroe to a heckler at the Lipton International Players Championship in Key Biscayne, Florida.

"**They say rugby is a beastly game played by gentlemen, soccer a gentleman's game played by beasts and football a beastly game played by beasts.**"

Henry Blaha, captain of the Baltimore Rugby Club.

"**A** racetrack is a place where windows clean people."

Danny Thomas, comic.

"**My wife made me a millionaire.
I used to have *three* million.**"

Bobby Hull, Hockey Hall of Famer, on his former wife.

"**F**ishing is a delusion entirely surrounded by liars in old clothes."

Don Marquis, humorist.